Can Teachers Own Their Own Schools?

Can Teachers Own Their Own Schools?

New Strategies for Educational Excellence

Richard K. Vedder

Foreword by Chester E. Finn, Jr.

The INDEPENDENT INSTITUTE

Oakland, California

The Independent Institute
100 Swan Way, Oakland, CA 94621-1428
Telephone: 510-632-1366 • Fax 510-568-6040
E-mail: info@independent.org
Website: http://www.independent.org

Library of Congress Control Number: 00-91200
ISBN: 0-945999-83-6

Published by The Independent Institute, a nonprofit, nonpartisan, scholarly research and educational organization that sponsors comprehensive studies on the political economy of critical social and economic issues. Nothing herein should be construed as necessarily reflecting the views of the Institute or as an attempt to aid or hinder the passage of any bill before Congress.

The INDEPENDENT INSTITUTE

The **Independent Institute** is the non-profit, non-partisan, scholarly research and educational organization that sponsors comprehensive studies on the political economy of critical social and economic problems.

The politicization of decision making in society has largely confined public debate to the narrow reconsideration of existing policies. Given the prevailing influence of partisan interests, little social innovation has occurred. In order to understand both the nature of and possible solutions to major public issues, The Independent Institute's program adheres to the highest standards of independent inquiry and is pursued regardless of prevailing political or social biases and conventions. The resulting studies are widely distributed as books and other publications, and publicly debated through numerous conference and media programs.

Through this uncommon independence, depth, and clarity, The Independent Institute pushes at the frontiers of our knowledge, redefines the debate over public issues, and fosters new and effective directions for government reform.

THE INDEPENDENT INSTITUTE
100 Swan Way, Oakland, CA 94621-1428, U.S.A.
Telephone: 510-632-1366 • Fax 510-568-6040
E-mail: info@independent.org • Website: http://www.independent.org

Table of Contents

Foreword

The Thomas B. Fordham Foundation is very pleased to co-sponsor with The Independent Institute the preparation and publication of this important and provocative study by Richard K. Vedder.

That does not mean we necessarily agree with all of the ideas set forth herein or are ready to see them embraced tomorrow by the entire country. But they deserve to be widely debated and tested.

Giving teachers an economic stake in the success of their schools is a terrific idea. Letting teachers (and other school staff) actually own their schools is also intriguing. Creating stronger, competitive incentives for school success is an important policy emphasis, recently underscored by the National Alliance of Business in its report, *Improving Performance: Competition in American Public Education*. Professor Vedder's wide-ranging and inventive study frames several approaches to accomplishing these worthy goals. That's why we are delighted to have this monograph circulating.

Some people will doubtless be uncomfortable with Vedder's proposal for school privatization, especially the suggestion that schools may charge tuition over and above the amount of the publicly funded "vouchers" that their students might receive. I'm wary myself, nervous that profit-maximizing schools may raise prices beyond the ability of low-income families to pay or look askance at "high-cost" youngsters with disabilities. Vedder doesn't think so, however, and points to historical and contemporary evidence that private schools serve needy children well. Skeptics may well respond that this evidence is too limited or from too distant a past to justify confidence.

All the more we should try it and see. We know that the education status quo is unacceptable, particularly for disadvantaged youngsters. Thus, I conclude about Professor Vedder's proposals, as about so many of today's proliferating education reform ideas, that we shouldn't just debate theories and "what ifs". We should encourage bona fide experimentation. Vedder's ideas deserve a proper field test at the community or state level.

Can that happen? The more time I spend in this field, the more appalled I become by the argument that no reform should even be tried unless and until its proponents can prove in advance that it will work perfectly and will have no adverse consequences or unwanted side effects. Of course, the people who make that argument never apply the same standard of perfection to the present failing system. As a result, the system is allowed to continue engaging in education malpractice—while proposed alternatives are blocked. I am also wary of the odor of anti-empiricism that accompanies this stance, the whiff of "we don't really want to know whether this will work; we're afraid to find out; hence we're better off ignorant."

Nobody yet has found a foolproof formula for revitalizing American K-12 education. So let's be humble enough—and empirical enough—to try as many tantalizing approaches as we can. In that spirit, I commend Richard Vedder's pioneering ideas for your consideration.

> Chester E. Finn, Jr.,
> President
> Thomas B. Fordham Foundation
> Washington, D.C.

1

Introduction

This Independent Policy Report examines the concept of employee-owned for-profit schools, showing that it is an idea with strong historical roots that was hastily discarded more than a century ago, despite evidence that it was improving literacy. For-profit education is again on the rise in America, and is a form of delivery that deserves serious consideration.

For at least the past two decades, there has been mounting concern that U.S. youth are being poorly educated. Americans fare poorly on international tests in math, science and other subjects. An education reform effort begun in the early 1980s has met with, at best, limited success in terms of improved student outcomes, despite a huge increase in resources devoted to public schooling. Educational efficiency (outcomes related to costs) has by many measures declined significantly.[1]

Piecemeal reforms such as strengthened teacher certification, merit pay, decentralized management, reduced class size, public-school choice and curricular innovation (e.g., whole language approach, block scheduling, Core Knowledge) have had limited impact. Accordingly, in recent years, attention has increasingly focused on the creation of new and more market-based approaches to delivering education services. In part, this has taken the form of increasing privatization of education with the use of public funds, such as the outsourcing of school services to private firms and proposals to use vouchers (scholarships) to allow students to attend private schools. A further approach has been charter schools, which seek to free public schools from many of the bureaucratic and regulatory restraints that inhibit education innovation. Finally, a growing number of parents have become so disenchanted with all

1

conventional schools that they have been teaching their children at home.

Historical and contemporary evidence suggest that for-profit education often yields improved student outcomes at reduced costs. Thus education productivity improves. The discipline and incentives of the marketplace lead to behavioral modification that promotes both learning and efficiency.

Another argument in support of for-profit education relates to the fact that other reform efforts (e.g., vouchers, independent charter schools, home schooling) have been fought bitterly by groups with a special interest in maintaining the status quo, including teacher unions, but in some cases also state department bureaucracies, PTAs, school boards and administrator organizations, etc. Opponents have generally succeeded in fending off vouchers, constraining charters and watering down other attempts at radical reform.

For-profit schools deal with this political problem by changing the delivery system in fundamental ways while simultaneously offering the potential of financial rewards for teachers and others who feel threatened by change. One approach is to make school employees (and perhaps others who are closely involved with the schools) part or full owners of privatized, for-profit corporations. In return for a transfer of wealth to these employees, they would be invited, tempted, or, under some scenarios, obliged to go along with a shift to competitive for-profit delivery systems. The method of transfer to private ownership might vary, but could well be similar to the Employee Stock Ownership Plans (ESOPs) that are commonplace in American business.

This study provides a detailed discussion of how ESOP-type schools might work, and identifies some of their problems and potential benefits. It shows that profit is not a new concept in U.S. schooling and that there are both historical precedents and contemporary examples of successful proprietary schools. It suggests that moving to an ESOP approach for primary and secondary education might approach what economists call "Pareto superiority," a situation where some people will be better off and no one is worse off than before. This cannot be determined for certain, however, without a serious and properly designed experiment with the ESOP approach.

2

American Education: Poor Outcomes and Declining Efficiency

By most indicators, American children, nearly 90 percent of whom attend government-operated public schools, learn less than their counterparts in other highly developed countries.[2] By some indicators, they learn less than they did thirty years ago, and even where there are signs of improvement in knowledge, they are small.[3] In the best case scenario, education outcomes have improved very modestly, while the costs of obtaining them have soared. Inputs (resources) are rising faster than outputs (student learning), so efficiency has declined. Even with the best case scenario, a large percentage of Americans at the completion of secondary schooling lack the skills needed in today's knowledge–intensive workplace. While recent experience may call the conclusion into question, at least one scholar has attributed America's productivity slowdown after 1973 to a decline in student academic performance.[4]

Figure 1 shows that from 1967 to 1997, the average composite SAT score fell in the United States. The drop was pronounced between 1967 and 1980, and then shows a partial recovery since. The math scores have risen more than verbal scores, which still languish well below the levels observed in 1967. ACT test scores showed a similar decline in the 1970s as well. The findings are not much better if one uses alternative indicators. For example, the National Assessment of Educational Progress (NAEP) has tested U.S. students for more than three decades at the fourth, eighth and twelfth grade levels. In reading, there have been very slight gains in average NAEP test scores from 1971 to 1996, but some of them (e.g., for seventeen-year-old students) have not been statistically significant.[5] The picture in math is much the same. International test comparisons show even more dismal results. For example, of the forty-one nations reporting eighth grade mathematics test scores on the Third International Mathematics and Science Study (TIMSS), the United States ranked 28th.

FIGURE 1
Composite Average SAT Scores 1967–97

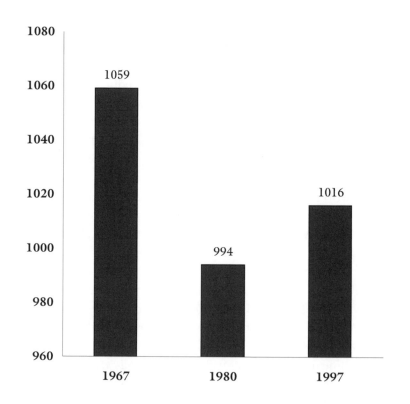

Source: U.S. Bureau of the Census, Statistical Abstract of the United States

The lackluster American education performance level is not because of a deprivation of resources. Figure 2 shows that real per pupil current spending in 1997 dollars in public schools (enrolling nearly 90 percent of all students) almost tripled from 1960 to 1997, and this gain is probably undersated due to the tendency for price indices to exaggerate inflation.[6] American spending on public schools is high relative to other nations, including countries whose students tend to outperform those in the United States. As Figure 3 shows, spending per pupil at the secondary level was significantly

FIGURE 2
Real Per Pupil Current Expenditures, 1960–97

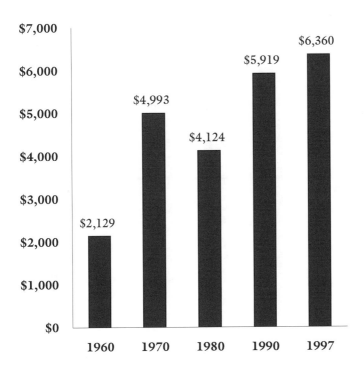

Source: From author's calculations using data from the National Center for Education Statistics

higher in the U.S. in 1994 than in such European nations as France or Sweden, and dramatically higher than in Korea or Hungary, nations that in general have students who outperform Americans.[7]

The data show that U.S. students fare poorly in school, that performance has changed little over time and that the costs of education are rising sharply and are high by international standards. This evidence, of course, does not prove that America's education delivery system is the culprit; perhaps the decline in the nuclear family, anti-intellectualism in American life, too much TV watching or other factors explain both the

FIGURE 3
Per Pupil Secondary School Spending, 1994

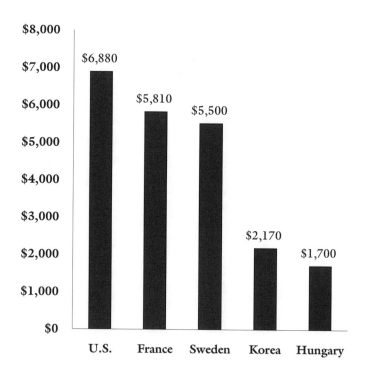

Source: From author's calculations using data from the National Center for Education Statistics

trends within the United States and the international comparisons. Nonetheless, taken alone this evidence lends support to those arguing that U.S. K–12 schooling is both ineffective and costly.

Other things being equal, this evidence strengthens the case for seeking new ways of promoting education and delivering education services. One such approach is the for-profit school, owned in part or whole by its employees, the so-called ESOP approach. We now turn to describing the theory of for-profit education and the advantages it offers to students, teachers and the public. We look at historical and contemporary evidence. We then examine several alternative methods by which such a system might be implemented.

3

Long Term Benefits
of the For-Profit Approach

Student Benefits

The for-profit approach largely replaces centralized bureaucratic control of schools with a decentralized delivery system where consumer choices enforce standards and accountability. In virtually every other field of human endeavor where private for-profit corporations have existed alongside publicly owned and managed business, the for-profit private businesses offer a superior product, often at a lower price. Thus Federal Express and United Parcel Service have captured a large amount of business from the U.S. Postal Service, and more people visit tourist attractions of the Disney Co. in Florida and California than National Park Service sites with great natural beauty such as the Grand Canyon.

These commercial successes reflect inherent advantages of the market approach. The discipline of the market provides incentives for producers to offer a high quality product, while economizing on the resources used. In education, several factors enter into customer satisfaction. Non-instructional factors are relevant and sometimes important, parents prefer to send their children to schools with successful sports teams, pleasant physical facilities, and a low incidence of crime. Most parents, however, are primarily interested in their children receiving a "high-quality education," by which they usually mean acquiring knowledge and academic skills.[8] A successful for-profit school must have satisfied customers, which means it must demonstrate that it is offering positive learning experiences to children.

First and foremost, for-profits must show their success by having students demonstrate learning skills on objective measures of performance, such as state tests and university entrance exams. Secondarily, the profit motive encourages schools to engage in curricular and institutional innovation. A successful school may attract students by offering state-of-the-art distance learning opportunities, by using traditional learning approaches favored by many parents (e.g., teaching phonics or multiplication tables) and by introducing foreign language instruction in early grades. Teaching what parents want taught, not what bureaucrats dictate, simultaneously increases consumer satisfaction and the school's financial success.

Benefits to Taxpayers

In the current public education environment, the costs of schooling are increased by the fact that few persons have much incentive to conserve on resources. There are no extra dividends or capital gains associated with reducing costs. The discipline of the market changes that, and in the long run increases incentives to run schools economically. Even in the non-profit sector, costs per private-school pupil tend to be well below those in public schools. In the long run, one would expect that for-profit private schools would tend to curb such costly practices as teacher tenure and extremely small class size and instead seek effective but more economical ways of providing instruction and minimizing such non-instructional costs as administration and transportation.

Benefits to Teachers

As discussed in detail below, a teacher receiving stock in a for-profit educational corporation might expect to derive substantial financial benefits. But finances aside, many teachers today are dissatisfied by the central control over their classrooms and their limited ability to select curriculum, discipline students and participate meaningfully in the school community. In a school substantially owned by teachers, this will work very differently. The sense of community is apt to be keen. We already know that teachers in private settings are more content with their working conditions, and the for-profit nature of the offering potentially could boost their satisfaction. It's also noteworthy that schools with a strong sense of community tend to have better academic performance.[9]

4

A Historical Perspective
on For-Profit Schools

The concept of for-profit schools goes back thousands of years. Andrew Coulson notes that in ancient Athens, schooling was private, with many instructors operating their schools on a for-profit basis.[10] The schools of Isocrates and Aspasia were well known, successful and distinctive (Isocrates's emphasizing practical knowledge and Aspasia's opening her doors to women). According to Coulson, Athens reached its pinnacle of cultural and economic success with a system of private schools, many of them operating on a for-profit basis, while Sparta languished under its system of government-run schools with a rigid curriculum and no parental choice.

Early in the nineteenth century, most people in Great Britain and the United States who were educated at all were educated privately, very often in schools operating for profit. In England, there was virtually no public support for education before 1830, and such support was very limited before 1870. This is interesting in that most economic historians believe the Industrial Revolution was effectively completed by the mid-nineteenth century.[11] Thus the powerful economic forces that led to the first sustained growth in income and output in world history were unleashed during a period when knowledge was transmitted from generation to generation by private means. As late as 1875, total education expenditures by the central and local governments in England and Wales were below five million pounds sterling, less than half of one percent of total output and less than one pound for every child between the ages of five and fourteen.[12]

The private schools took many forms. A large number of students attended small schools operated by teacher-entrepreneurs whose income came from the tuition collected. In some schools, private philanthropy created endowments to fund some or even all education costs. But, as Adam Smith noted in 1776, "the endowments of schools and colleges have necessarily diminished more or less the necessity of application in the teachers."[13] In other words, where the income of teachers was solely dependent on payments made by the customers (the students), they tended to apply themselves more.

Despite government's absence, Britain's education participation and attainment levels both advanced. From 1818 to 1834, school enrollments soared from 478,000 to 1,294,000.[14] In 1840, probably nearly two-thirds of English adults could read and/or write, while by 1870 that proportion had reached at least 75–80 percent.[15] So even before there was significant governmental involvement in education, most people learned to read and/or write and voluntary participation in schooling was on the rise.

David Mitch has analyzed the impact of public versus private schools on literacy in England, and concluded that the private schools seemed to impact quite positively on both men and women, in contrast to public schools.[16] This is consistent with an observation by Adam Smith more than two centuries earlier: "Those parts of education, it is to be observed, for the teaching of which there are no publick institutions, are generally the best taught."[17]

The picture in the United States is more complex, owing to the federal structure and the variation among states. New England became fairly heavily involved with public schooling even in the colonial era, but most states in the new nation had largely private education in the early nineteenth century. Many schools were in fact hybrids, nominally private institutions with some public funding. For example, in the 1820s in New York City there was a Free School Society that received some tax monies and served broad public purpose, but it was privately run and controlled. For every student in a Society school, there were three in private schools, many of them run for profit.[18] As in England, public schools were considered necessary only to supplement private ones, mainly in rural areas with few schools. The New York Commissioners of the Common Schools reported in 1812 that: "In populous cities, and the parts of the country thickly settled, schools are generally established by individual exertion."[19]

In the second quarter of the nineteenth century, the common or public school movement became popular throughout much of the nation. Still, as late as 1850, more funds for American education came from private sources than from government. By 1870, about two-thirds of all financial resources were publicly provided.[20] Most scholars attribute this increased public involvement to Horace Mann, who became secretary of the Massachusetts Board of Education in 1837, or to Henry Barnard, another early advocate of free public schools. Education historians have offered several different interpretations as to why this movement began.[21] The traditional view, enunciated by Ellwood Cubberley and Merle Curti, is that common schools would extend the franchise to many more people, consistent with American egalitarian ideals and democratic values.[22] The common school was designed, according to this view, to promote equal opportunity and to allow society's have nots to enjoy benefits available to the more affluent. By giving ultimate control over schools to states (instead of localities), it was said, the nation would develop shared values and reduce geographic inequities. The advocates of common schools generally favored an expansive role for the state and downplayed individual responsibility and the ability of markets to make intelligent decisions about the investment of human capital.

Revisionist writers have challenged this view of the common-school movement. Historian Carl Kaestle noted that common-school advocates were mostly Protestants of Anglo-Saxon origins, and that the common-school movement coincided with a rise in mass immigration, much of it consisting of Roman Catholics from Ireland and other countries. Kaestle argues that the common schools were designed to provide a foundation for preserving and extending Anglo-American Protestant and capitalistic values.[23] An even more radical interpretation comes from Michael Katz. While he shares Kaestle's view on the religious and ideological motive, he also contends that the common-school movement was "a coalition of the social leaders, status-anxious parents, and status-hungry educators to impose educational innovation, each for their own reasons, upon a reluctant community."[24] This is precisely what Herbert Spencer, writing during the midst of the American common-school movement predicted would happen in England if it adopted public schools: "We may be quite sure that a state education would be administered for the advantage of those in power rather than for the advantage of the nation."[25]

Much historical research calls into question the legitimacy of some of the early arguments for public schools. Kaestle, looking at New York *private* schools in the 1790s, noted significant differences in the social backgrounds of students. As Joel Spring has put it, "private schools were attended by a variety of children from different social classes because a practice existed of adjusting tuition according to the income of the parents."[26] The rise of public schools led to a change in the nature of private school enrollments, making them more a haven for the wealthy. Consequently, governmental schooling may well have *reduced*, not increased, the "democratic" dimension of American education, at least as practiced in New York. Regarding overall attendance, Kaestle found little difference between the level of participation of students attending largely free public schools in the mid-1800s with those attending the private schools of the 1790s. In an important book co-authored with Maris Vinovskis, he observed that the common-school movement did not lead to increased education participation in Massachusetts, with the percent of the population under twenty attending school showing little change from 1840 to 1880.[27] The notion that public schools enhanced the social mixing of young people and increased educational opportunities is accordingly highly suspect.

Lawrence Cremin's book provides some 1850 data that let me further test the proposition that public schooling widened education participation.[28] Using multiple regression analysis for the northern United States, I find no statistically significant positive relationship between school attendance and public funding. My findings are consistent with those of Kaestle and Vinovskis, namely that the big push for public funding of schools was not accompanied by a surge in participation in the education system.

In the century after the triumph of the "free" public school, private education in the United States continued to exist, primarily in non-profit settings. The largest proportion of students attended religious schools, especially those run by the Roman Catholic Church. A smaller number attended high quality non-sectarian schools. For a variety of reasons, Catholic enrollments began to decline after the early 1960s, which briefly led to some fall-off in the proportion of students attending private schools. In recent years, however, that trend has reversed. Non-Catholic religious-oriented schools enjoyed rapid increases in enrollments in the 1970s and 1980s, and the decline in Catholic enrollments has likewise stopped.

The most explosive growth in private education, however, has come in the area of home schooling, which probably now accounts for almost three percent of K–12 enrollments, up from a fraction of one percent a generation ago. In 1990, about 300,000 children probably received home schooling.[29] By 1996, their number probably neared 1 million, i.e. 2 percent of total enrollments.[30] Annual growth approached 20 percent per year. Assuming enrollment growth has slowed to, say, 10 percent per year, the number of children currently being home schooled is probably about 1.3 million, more than quadruple the number at the beginning of the 1990s. In addition, the modern era has witnessed a small but growing number of for-profit proprietary schools within the private education sector. All told, the non-public component of education now probably approaches 12–13 percent of total enrollments, an increase from a decade ago despite the sharp rise in subsidies to public institutions.[31] In addition, many other children are receiving supplemental instruction outside the public school setting from for-profit providers like Sylvan Learning Centers. Thus private education is gaining market share even without major voucher programs or other forms of government support.

5

For-Profit Education
in America Today

Skeptics of for-profit education might argue that this is an untried approach that, however appealing in theory, has no basis in experience. That is not actually true, however. For-profit schooling not only has ample historical precedent in the United States, it is arguably the fastest growing form of education delivery today. While it is true that relatively few of these ventures are K–12 schools in precisely the manner described below, they contain many of the attributes that would be common to K–12 for-profit schools.

In an Internet search in late summer 1999, I identified twenty-two listed U.S. companies whose primary business is providing education services. That excludes some prominent firms not listed on a stock exchange at that time. For example, Edison Schools has subsequently gone public and now has a market capitalization of nearly $500 million. Moreover, the list excludes many companies providing education supplies and materials, such as textbook publishers. The twenty-two companies operated at all levels of education, from preschool to postgraduate. They had combined sales exceeding $3.9 billion during the previous year, up 21.9 percent over the previous year. Their market capitalization was an impressive $7.4 billion (nearly double sales revenue), with valuations indicating that investors viewed them as growth firms with significant future increases in earnings likely. According to Yahoo Finance, the companies in its "schools" group have had an earnings increase over the past five years that is more than double the average of companies in the Standard and Poor's 500-stock index.

Broadening the definition of "education company" to include corporations providing supplies, transportation and food services, etc., leads to an even larger assessment of this industry's size. One estimate places market capitalization at $12 billion (as of June 30, 1999).[32] Moreover, one projection by stock market analysts predicts 24.9 percent annual earnings growth between 1999 and 2004, compared with 7 percent for the broad-based S & P 500.[33] A few of the major for-profit companies include the Apollo Group (operating the University of Phoenix), Sylvan Learning Systems (operating Sylvan Learning Centers, testing programs, etc.), and DeVry, Inc. (technical programs, Becker CPA Review). Several for-profits operate in the more traditional K–12 market, including Edison Schools, Nobel Learning and The Tesseract Group. While these latter companies have a mixed record of financial success, some of them have recorded excellent results as far as student performance is concerned. Tesseract, for example, reports very good results in Arizona with student achievement in recent months relative to the average for the state (Figure 4). While the composite average score on the reading, math and language tests was 52.3 for all Arizona students, it was higher in the relatively new (and culturally diverse) Tesseract charter schools and much higher at the Tesseract-run private school.[34] While other factors may be at work, the evidence seems to be that the company is offering a high quality education.

As of this writing, several significant ventures in K–12 education are closely held firms whose stock is not traded publicly. Most of these smaller companies are likely to go public at some future date. For example, The Leona Group manages twenty-five schools, while National Heritage Academies runs fourteen schools with "back-to-basics education with a religious tinge."[35] Two famous businessmen, ex-junk bond king Michael Milken and Oracle CEO Larry Ellison, are investing in for-profits via their private holding company, Knowledge Universe.

The growth in charter schools also provides a vehicle for private firms to enter public funded education, either through direct ownership of such schools, or by signing management contracts with independent charter boards to operate such schools. One respected market analyst, Michael T. Moe of Merrill Lynch, predicts that education management companies will handle 10 percent of K–12 public school spending within ten to fifteen years.[36] Moreover, traditional education suppliers such as textbook companies are considering entering the business of providing direct instructional services. Harcourt General has announced plans to begin an on-line university and UOL Publishing adapts college courses for the Internet, an approach that can easily be transferred to K–12 students attending publicly funded schools, private schools or to home-schooled children.

FIGURE 4
Stanford 9 Test Scores, Spring 1999

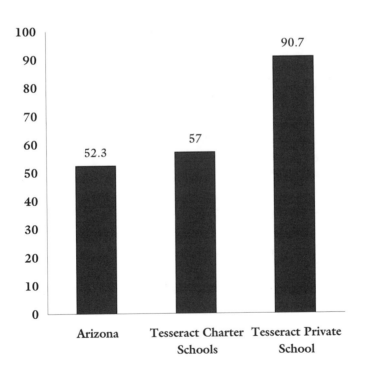

Source: 1999 Annual Report of the Tesseract Group, Inc.

Private School Performance

In general, private schools have higher levels of student performance and lower expenditure levels than public schools. Recently released student performance data from Ohio are fairly typical. On that state's ninth-grade proficiency test examination administered in the fall of 1999, required of all students in both public and private schools, 41 percent of the public school children failed at least one of the five parts of the test, about double the proportion, 21 percent, for private school children. On the mathematics exam, 32 percent of public school children failed, compared with 14 percent of private school children.[37] Studies of Catholic high schools consistently show that compared to the public schools they put a greater emphasis on academics and achieve higher student test scores, even after controlling for other factors such as family background.[38] Moreover, the national evidence is that on average private schools achieve more with far lower costs than public schools. As one writer put it, "The simple fact is that the average independent school costs half as much per pupil as the average public school."[39]

In recent years a limited number of public and private voucher plans have begun operation. The demand for these vouchers far exceeds the supply. The Children's Scholarship Fund, which offers vouchers for poor urban students in grades K–8, received a million applications for the 44,000 vouchers they had available. Surely this is a sign of the great demand for private education especially among those forced to attend the worst public schools.[40] The most extensive experiment with using public funds to finance private school education has occurred in Milwaukee, which began offering vouchers to students several years ago. As with the private scholarship plans, the Milwaukee plan had far more applicants than vouchers and recipients were thus assigned randomly. The random choice of recipients is a boon to researchers who can compare the achievement of those students who receive vouchers with those that remain in the public schools. Studies using this method have found that randomly chosen students do better in private than in public schools. For example, Harvard's Paul Peterson and associates have found positive student outcomes in both math and reading arising from the voucher experience.[41] Cecilia E. Rouse of the National Bureau of Economic Research finds significant improvement on math performance (but not reading) in her appraisal.[42] The evidence is not unanimous. One state-funded study of the voucher experiment, which many scholars think is flawed because it did not compare randomly chosen students, found no gains.[43] Overall the evidence shows that private schools outperform public schools and they do so at lower cost. The studies of the Milwaukee voucher program, which is in its infancy, are consistent with these results. On balance these studies find positive learning effects from private schools even after controlling for other important factors.

6

Illustrating The "ESOP" Approach to Public Education

I now turn to the question of how to get from a government run schooling system to an entrepreneurial, for-profit system. The essence of the idea is to privatize the school by giving its ownership to its teachers, principals and staff. Other stakeholders—notably parents—might also receive ownership rights (stock) in the new corporation. Alternatively the schools could be sold to existing for-profit corporations with a proviso that teachers, principals, and other stakeholders receive substantial stock in them. To be clear, I run through a detailed example.

Assume that a city of 25,000 people chooses to implement a market-oriented approach to education delivery that gives considerable power to consumers, i.e. students and parents, rather than to producers, namely the traditional school system. Suppose further that there are 4,000 students attending public schools in the community, 2,000 of whom are in kindergarten through sixth grade at five elementary schools. Let us assume that 400 students attend each school: Washington, Adams, Jefferson, Madison and Monroe. Let us suppose that the district has $6 million in bonded indebtedness, $2 million of which is attributable to two of the elementary schools, and that it anticipates having $2 million in cash on hand at the end of the current fiscal year. Suppose that the district's operating budget, including debt service, is $20 million, with estimated costs per pupil of $4,000 in grades K–6, and $6,000 in grades 7–12 (with central office expenses prorated between the two groups).

Suppose the district announces that it plans to give its elementary schools to five new for-profit companies that it will help organize.

Each corporation will operate one school. The district announces that it will give 100 shares of the relevant common stock to each teacher for each year of service to the district, with 200 shares to the principal for each year of service, 100 shares per year for other members of the professional staff (e.g., librarians, nurses, guidance counselors), and 50 shares per year for support staff (secretaries, paid teacher aides, bus drivers, custodians, etc).

Using Washington School as an example, suppose it has twenty-two teachers with an average of fifteen years experience. They would receive 33,000 shares collectively in the new corporation (22 X 100 X 15). The principal, with twenty years of experience, would receive 4,000 shares (200 X 20), and presumably would be the initial chief executive officer (CEO) of the corporation. Suppose another 12,000 shares go to other employees as outlined above. The central district, with perhaps a dozen administrative persons in its central office (superintendent, assistant superintendent, curriculum coordinator, transportation supervisor, gifted specialists, etc.) might encourage one person to go to work for each corporation, both to pare down the district office staff which now will only directly serve 2,000 students in grades 7–12, and also to provide added staff at the building level to do things previously centralized.

All told, employees are given 49,000 shares of Washington School Corporation. Suppose another 31,000 shares are sold to the public at $25 per share, raising a total of $775,000 in capital. Assuming the same formula applies to the other four corporations, the district will raise $3,875,000 from the sale of stock, of which it will use $2 million to retire the debt on elementary school buildings and give the remaining cash to each corporation ($375,000 apiece) as operating capital. Presumably, first priority will be given to residents of the district to buy stock, and in particular parents would be encouraged to do so. Suppose that, at Washington school, 150 parents bought on average 100 shares apiece, or 15,000 of the 31,000 shares sold to the public. Some employees might buy additional shares, and the remainder would be sold to the general public. On balance, slightly over 60 percent of the corporation will be owned by its employees, nearly 20 percent by parents, and nearly 20 percent by other members of the public.

What are owners of the stock getting? The school's real estate would be turned over to the corporation, together with existing equipment and supplies. Suppose the Washington School building and its equipment were worth $2 million. Thus the property alone would have a book value of $25 per share ($2 million divided by 80,000 shares). In addition, the corporation would receive $375,000 in cash from the district, worth almost $5 more per share, giving the corporation a book value of nearly $30 per share. The IPO (initial public offering) price of $25, then, would represent a discount from the underlying value of the stock, reflecting the inherent risk in a new venture.

Most important, the Washington School Corporation receives a contract with the school district stating that the district will honor payment vouchers presented to Washington by parents of students attending the school. These vouchers in the first year would be worth $4,000 (the district's cost of educating children). To ease investor anxiety about the continuation of the revenue flow, the district might agree to a five or seven year plan of voucher payments to each school corporation, with the per pupil amounts rising by not less than the amount of inflation, or alternatively, by a percentage equal to the increase in per pupil spending at the schools where students in grades seven through twelve attend.

Washington School would also be free to charge whatever tuition fees it wants. If it sets the fee at $4,000, it will receive $4,000 in reimbursement from the school district for each student, and each parent will pay nothing, as at present. Suppose Washington School is considered the best school in town, however, and gets 450 applicants, of which it can handle only 400 due to physical capacity constraints. It might choose to raise its tuition to $4,200, providing opportunities for profit.[44] By contrast, Adams School may be in a tough neighborhood and only get 350 initial applicants. To encourage more applications, including those rejected at Washington School, teachers at Adams might agree to teach a half hour longer each day, offering fifty minutes more weekly instruction in reading, math and science.

As part of the agreement setting up for-profit schools, the employees must agree at the start that collective bargaining agreements with the former employer (the school district) are null and void. The stock given to teachers would have a market value that would entice them to support such a move. For example, an influential senior teacher at Jefferson with twenty-four years of experience would receive 2,400 shares valued at $60,000 (at the $25 per share IPO price), equivalent to one to two years of salary. It might be necessary, in order to secure teacher approval, to guarantee that first year salaries would equal what they otherwise would have been had the school remained public. In such a circumstance, teachers would be receiving a material addition to their wealth with no loss of income. They would be trading off the lifetime job security afforded under the old arrangement for a significant increase in their wealth plus greater say in how the school will operate.

In addition, there has to be agreement at the state level that the new school is exempt from most government regulations dealing with such matters as class size, teacher certification, tenure, uniform salary schedules, etc. If the new school is to behave differently than the old one, it must be free to change.

Over time, schools would adopt strategies designed to increase revenues and reduce costs, so as to make profits and further increase wealth derived from the stock.[45] Washington School might adopt a highly traditional curriculum using phonics and the Core Knowledge sequence. It might raise its tuition, requiring some parental financial contribution beyond that provided by the voucher. Adams school might cut its costs by privatizing bus transportation, food and maintenance and by hiring new teachers at salaries below the old scale. They might price their tuition slightly below the amount of the voucher, allowing parents to get a cash refund (e.g., if the district provides $4,000 in voucher aid, and tuition is set at $3,800, each parent will receive $200 in cash). It will market itself as the low cost alternative. Jefferson School might try to lure a superstar teacher away from Washington and brag about this in its publicity to parents. It might also emphasize the arts. Madison might introduce non-denominational Christian teachings as a feature of its instruction, while Monroe might stress student freedom of expression and experiential learning.

In short, in order to expand its revenues, each school will alter its curriculum and perhaps its price in order to attract more students. Each will likely push students to do well on standardized tests, since good test performance would be an excellent marketing tool. (The state or local testing authority will, of course, have to ensure test security so as to minimize the incidence of cheating.) If a school has a high-priced teacher who is ineffective in the classroom, the administration, supported by teacher-stockholders, will seek to ease him or her into retirement or alternative employment. If they can get rid of ineffective teacher X who costs, with benefits, $50,000 a year, and instead engage new and effective teacher Y, who costs $30,000, they increase profits by $20,000 while improving the instructional program, and attracting more students. The teachers, rather than having a union to shield the incompetent, will now monitor the effectiveness of their colleagues, anxious to improve the reputation and financial well-being of a business with which they have invested a sizable fraction of their net worth.

One area where the ESOP approach should lead to reductions in costs is class size. Other things being equal, teachers prefer small classes. It is easier and less tiring to educate eighteen students than twenty–five, for example. Teachers thus push for smaller class size, arguing that this has positive learning advantages. Yet the empirical evidence is strong that class size reduction has extremely small effects on learning.[46] Moreover, it is extremely expensive.

When teachers have a financial stake in reducing costs, they may see the possibility of increasing profits and stock prices by reducing staff and enlarging classes. To counter their competitor's claims that "X School has large classes," the school might incorporate low cost aides to assist teachers; it is $80,000 cheaper to hire sixteen teachers at an average annual cost of $40,000 along with eight teacher aides (bringing total staff in the classroom to twenty–four) at $20,000 a year then to hire twenty-two teachers. The ratio of staff to students would rise by using more aides, even though costs would fall somewhat. (If classes get too large to suit parents, however, enrollments will falter, thus creating a natural, marketplace brake on overdoing this approach to cost-cutting.)

An Alternative Approach

The illustration above assumes that the school district works with school personnel to establish the new school corporations. As noted earlier, there are already dozens of for-profit companies in the business of education. It might make sense for school boards to sell schools to existing corporations, such as Sylvan Learning or Edison Schools. To foster competition, however, it is imperative that not all schools be sold to the same provider.

Suppose Edison Schools buys the Washington School, paying $2 million to the district for the building, equipment and supplies and assuming some of the district's existing debt. Again, the district agrees to include Washington School in the aforementioned voucher program for a period of not less than five years. This approach would provide a financial windfall for the district; if all five schools were sold, it would receive $10 million. However, this plan would not provide stock for employees and would almost certainly precipitate legal action and work stoppages, particularly if the new private owners argued that the old collective bargaining agreements were null and void. To get teachers and other employees to go along, the District might agree to provide them with two choices. First, they could receive a severance payment in cash equal to $2,500 for each year taught, with similar provision for other employees (e.g., $1,250 for non-professional staff per year of service, $5,000 for the principal for each year, etc). If cash is taken, the teacher has no guarantee of continued employment with Edison Schools. A second option would be for the school district to use its funds to buy Edison stock in an ESOP trust (discussed below) in the name of teachers, using a formula similar to the one outlined above (e.g., $2,500 in stock for each year of service), with the teachers guaranteed employment at Edison at their existing salary for a year or two. Teachers not wanting to participate in a for-profit environment would receive a generous cash payment to retire, while those who stay would have a financial interest in the system. Obviously, Edison Schools (or whoever) would have to agree to these terms as a condition of purchase. The more substantial the job security provisions for existing teachers, the less attractive the school would be to potential purchaser/operators.

This approach has both advantages and disadvantages over the initial approach above. It may be advantageous to sell the school to an organization with management expertise in the for-profit environment. There may be economies of scale that would allow a large corporation to offer some services, such as technology, at far lower cost than if the school were part of a small local company. Also, this approach gives teachers an option: they can choose not to participate, leaving only those committed to trying the new system.

On the negative side, this approach reduces the financial consequences to the teachers when the school performs poorly. While teachers have a financial interest in Edison Schools, which leads to some sense of corporate loyalty and collegiality, if the Washington School founders while the other 150 or 200 Edison Schools flourish, the teachers will not feel a sense of financial loss for Washington's lack of success; in this case, if it can't turn the school around in a reasonable period, Edison would likely seek to sell it to someone else.[47]

Moreover, the sense of school community may be sharply reduced if teachers are part of a large corporation, much as if they are part of a large school district. The ability of local teachers to run their own affairs (e.g., picking textbooks and establishing discipline procedures) would be somewhat impaired, unless Edison in its wisdom gives them a high degree of local autonomy. If economies of scale and managerial expertise are important however, in the long run, localized school corporations likely will sell out to chains, much as hospitals, banks and other local institutions have in the past.

A Second Alternative Approach

The two approaches outlined above are not the only possible models. For example, suppose our mythical school district decides to create five elementary charter schools rather than five private corporations. Suppose the board of one of the charter schools, say Washington School, decides to contract out all education services to an education management company, say Advantage Schools or Edison Schools. It insists, as part of its contract, that preference be given to existing teachers in staffing the new school.

The provider then offers the teachers two options. The first allows employees to continue with the school for a year at the salary provided in the (former) collective bargaining agreement, which actually means a raise according to the (former) salary schedule and contract provisions. If the teacher selects this option, however, there is no guarantee of subsequent employment after this year, or of future salary increases. Alternatively, teachers can forego the built-in salary increase and instead receive stock in the service provider with a current value equal to the foregone salary increase or stock options exercisable over several years to buy a significant number of shares of the provider's stock at the current market price. Should the teacher select the second choice, he or she would be guaranteed employment for two years, instead of one under the first option. Still another variant on this idea would be to tie teachers' incremental compensation to the financial performance of that school (as opposed to the entire corporation); this is a profit-sharing variant to the equity participation approach.

One advantage of the charter approach is that it may be possible to circumvent some political and legal obstacles to teacher-owned schools. If a strong charter law negates existing collective bargaining agreements for "conversion" schools, this approach is an excellent way of moving towards teacher-owned schools. Teachers would be given options, and those devoid of any interest in equity participation would be given an out, though they will also have ample financial incentives to participate. At the same time, the ephemeral nature of the management contract between the school board and the school provider may add uncertainty and make teachers apprehensive about participation.

Transition Issues

Financial Concerns

While the hypothetical school district in our examples estimated the cost of educating an elementary pupil at $4,000, its calculations were likely based on accounting procedures that do not pass muster in the private sector. Specifically, many public school districts use a cash accounting approach, certainly not the generally accepted accounting principles (GAAP) universally used in the private sector. For example, school districts typically do not expense the depreciation of buildings and equipment (e.g., writing off computers in three years, for example).

The new private schools will also face two other expenses that public school monopolies do not have: taxes and marketing costs. It would not be uncommon for, say, Washington School to face an annual $25,000 bill for property taxes. To ease transition, it is possible that municipal property tax abatement might be granted to the new schools for, say, five years. This is analogous to what local governments often do with many private businesses making new investments—and of course the municipality is not accustomed to property tax revenues from the Washington School building. Since property taxes are likely going largely to finance schools in any case, an argument can be made to exempt them, at least in the short run.[48]

The evidence from for-profit educational institutions currently in existence is that advertising and marketing costs often reach 10 percent of total revenues. While the total for schools in mid-size towns or cities probably would be considerably less, there would still be a material expense relating to advertising, recruiting and processing applications. Critics of school choice might consider this a wasteful expense. An alternative interpretation is that advertising helps consumers make informed choices and these marketing expenses are the cost of moving from monopolies that disregard consumer wants to a system of choice which allows them to buy the service, in this case schooling, that best suits them.

Nonetheless, over time, schools would have to budget for marketing expense. In the very short run, they would likely use some of their initial cash balances to finance a modest marketing campaign. Over time, outlays for marketing may expand as schools allocate resources for this purpose.

Longer term, it is likely that the public cost of education would fall, or at least that the rate of increase would decline. The discipline of market incentives should end some wasteful practices of public schools. Over the long run, public authorities trying to reduce governmental expenditures might insist that well-to-do parents pay more educational costs themselves (e.g., they would receive a smaller voucher), entrusting more of the financial responsibility for education to the parent rather than the state. The full advantage of market-based education is not realized when third parties (e.g., the government) pay the bills rather than consumers. Consumers will become more price-sensitive and thereby force greater efficiencies to the extent that they pay a portion of the bills themselves. This is no doubt a factor in the substantially lower costs observed in private religious schools. To avoid the problem which have afflicted the health-care market, where third-party payments have led to soaring costs, the longer term objective should be to reduce the component of tuition charges paid for by the government.

Of course opponents of radical education reform can be expected to fiercely oppose any scheme that raises the possibility of partial parental financial support. In the political give-and-take that would surround the adoption of any for-profit approach to public provision of education services, it might be necessary to prohibit new providers from raising tuition more than the amount of the voucher or scholarship for a period of some years. Such a provision reduces the potential profitability of for-profit schools, of course, and should be granted only if absolutely necessary to begin a for-profit experiment.

Some "equity" concerns of skeptics of the voucher/for-profit approach could be addressed in the initial contract between the public school district and the new for-profit companies. For example, larger vouchers would likely be necessary for disabled children, given the relatively higher cost of educating them. An argument can be made to provide larger vouchers for those from disadvantaged backgrounds (as evidenced by low family income, very low levels of parental education, or the absence of one or both parents from the home). By providing incremental amounts over the standard voucher for the disadvantaged, any argument that this approach favors the affluent is mitigated.

In the initial example, funds for the vouchers come from the local school district, presumably using a combination of state and local funds. Other funding options may be open. For example, a reform-minded federal and/or state government might wish to provide voucher funding for several years to several communities through demonstration grants, reducing the effectiveness of local opposition to the approach.

A final financial issue relates to the tax treatment of providing shares in a for-profit corporation to employees. This would ordinarily be considered income for the employees, exposing them to a significant federal income tax liability. However, if stock is held by an ESOP trust (discussed below), those tax problems might be reduced if not eliminated, although no doubt an IRS ruling and possibly federal tax law changes may be necessary to clarify this.

School Personnel

Public school systems typically face far more constraints in hiring than do private schools. For example, public school teachers ordinarily require a state teaching certificate while that is typically not the case for private schools. There is little empirical evidence suggesting that the courses needed for a teacher certificate have any impact on teacher effectiveness.[49] Thus the removal of such barriers would greatly increase the supply of potential teachers. A private school might simply require that all its teachers be college graduates who have not committed a felony, or possibly might hire college graduates who have successfully completed a program of practice teaching under the guidance of an experienced teacher.

The evidence is that private school teachers on balance are more satisfied with their jobs, even though their average pay is less than that earned by their public school counterparts. For example, in one recent survey, over 81 percent of private school teachers indicated that they were recognized for a job well done, compared with less than 68 percent in public schools.[50] The removal of a host of rules and restrictions should improve teacher morale, and more importantly in the long run, should widen the supply of teachers. This will ease pressures to increase teacher pay. Teachers will trade off some immediate income for non-pecuniary gains in terms of increased job satisfaction plus added wealth in the form of stock. In the long run, this should lower the cost of educating Americans and also increase public willingness to participate in efforts to improve student learning (after school programs, summer school, more technology for schools, etc).[51] Private schools presumably can discipline students more vigorously, and can take action against teachers who do not fulfill their responsibilities. Moreover, private for-profit schools would have incentives to deviate from the teacher pay schedules determined solely by years of experience and educational attainment. They could withhold tenure because of the substantial financial commitment involved, preferring to offer teachers one year or multi-year contracts, much as private schools do now.

One intricate transition issue relates to fringe benefits, particularly retirement. Public school teachers may be leaving a generous state retirement system a few years shy of receiving full benefits. It may be desirable to permit them to retain membership in the old system until they retire. In principle, for most teachers it should be possible to provide annuities, 401(k) defined contribution plans, etc., at least equal in value to the cost of the previous benefit, and the teacher can retire, perhaps receiving a modest public employee pension as well as a second pension from the private school. Indeed, since many public employee retirement schemes are defined benefit plans, by allowing teachers to enroll in a defined contribution private plan the teacher may receive more control over his or her retirement funds, greater choice and possibly a better return. In some states, the privatization of schools would, under current law, force teachers into the federal Social Security System. Again, it might be desirable to seek an amendment to the Social Security Act to give at least temporary respite from Social Security for senior employees a few years away from retirement.

Curricular Issues

Typically, school districts have a common curriculum for all schools in the system, and must often follow state guidelines as well. As schools withdraw from the public district, they must decide if and how to revise their curriculum—and the state or district must decide how much freedom they will have in this domain. For philosophical or marketing reasons, schools may wish to lengthen the school day or year, increasing coverage of some subjects, but not others. They also have to decide whether to follow a pedagogy previously favored by the unified district (e.g., the whole language approach to reading instruction), or abandon it for another approach. Other issues relate to team vs. individual teaching, and the extent to which the school wants to use technology. Since different schools are likely to reach somewhat different conclusions on all of these matters, the end result likely will be greater diversity in curricular matters. This, in turn, offers parents greater choices for their children.

A good case can nonetheless be made that new for-profit schools should remain subject to state academic standards and tests. Test data are necessary in assessing the validity of the for-profit concept in public education. Information provided by such tests assists parents in making rational school choices. State academic standards are important in having a citizenry which has a common education background, consistent with the democratic ideals espoused by many participants in the education reform debate. Politically, requiring the for-profit schools to comply with state standards and testing would raise the comfort level of persons of good will who are skeptical but not strongly hostile to experimenting with this approach.

Political/Legal Issues

In our original example, an individual school board decides to create private for-profit schools and finance the tuition payments of students attending them. In most states, that would require legislative approval. Teacher union leaders would surely oppose even a limited experiment as outlined above, arguing "education is about learning, not making money" or "this will promote state support of religion" or "this will destroy the democratic ideal of the common school," etc. National Education Association president Bob Chase, who dismisses for-profit schooling as another reform fad, argues that "educating children is very different from producing a product,"[52] Given the substantial financial and political clout of teacher unions, it will be difficult to overcome these objections. At the same time, the proposal offers tangible incentives for teachers themselves: tens of thousands of dollars worth of stock, the gaining of considerable control over curriculum, discipline, hiring, etc. and an attendant reduction in bureaucracy and regulation.

As stated above, enabling legislation must provide that newly created private schools be free from regulation in much the same manner as today's private schools. Public employee bargaining laws must be explicitly held not to apply, as teachers would no longer be public employees. The for-profit school employees would, of course, be subject to the National Labor Relations Act and other such laws that provide a framework within which workers can seek collective bargaining if they wish.

The Growth In Employee Stock Ownership in the U.S.

The notion of encouraging employees to take an ownership interest in the firm for which they work is not novel. By 1998, Federal Reserve data show that almost half of American families directly or indirectly owned stocks in business enterprises.[53] That compares with only 31.6 percent as late as 1989.[54] The growth in mutual funds, 401(k) plans, and Individual Retirement Accounts (IRAs) accounted for much of the rise. Clearly the most relevant development for this paper, however, was the growth in employee stock ownership of major companies. In part, this reflects a booming new movement at large American firms like PepsiCo and Starbucks to emulate high-tech firms like Microsoft by granting rank-and-file workers stock options.[55] Other firms match employee contributions to purchase company stock as part of savings or retirement plans.

An important and relevant innovation has been Employee Stock Ownership Plans, or ESOPs. The ESOP approach was the brainchild of a successful San Francisco attorney, Dr. Louis O. Kelso (1913–1991), who perfected the idea in the mid-1950s.[56] The Kelso approach found a powerful supporter in former U.S. Senator Russell Long, longtime chairman of the Senate Finance Committee. Long helped pass legislation providing favorable tax status to ESOP plans. By 1996, there were around 10,000 ESOP plans in operation, involving more than 10 million workers. A spate of recent favorable books on this approach has helped to make these plans better known and to enhance their popularity.[57]

A company wanting to set up an ESOP typically creates a trust to which it makes annual contributions. Each employee is allocated shares that the trust purchases, with the allocation based on various means (compensation, years of service, etc). Employees often have to wait several years before their ownership rights are fully vested. At age fifty-five, each employee must be given the option of diversifying up to 25 percent of his or her account; a one-time 50 percent diversification option occurs at age sixty. Employees receive the vested value of their assets when they leave the company, die, or retire. Provisions exist so employees can sell their shares when they are distributed to them.

ESOP plans have certain tax advantages, and often use leveraging techniques to give employees a substantial initial stock interest. In a leveraged ESOP, a bank will make a loan to an ESOP, with the loan guaranteed by the company. The ESOP uses the loan to buy either new or existing shares of company stock. The company makes annual payments to the ESOP, providing funds to repay the loan. When employees retire or otherwise leave the company, they take out their ESOP contribution either in cash or in shares of company stock.

ESOPs also have several tax advantages that are partially immaterial to public school districts, but other dimensions of the plans are appealing. The use of an ESOP trust avoids problems with direct employee ownership, including the quick sale of stock received by employees during initial formation of the company. The gradual vesting of ownership rights provides workers with incentives to stay through the transition from public to private ownership. Employees unfamiliar with direct ownership might find some solace in the collective ownership of stock, and the use of a trust probably enhances employee influence or even control of the company.

The ESOP experience at United Airlines (UAL Inc.) is perhaps relevant. In 1991 and 1992, UAL lost nearly $1.3 billion.[58] During 1993, the company, fighting for survival, introduced stringent cost-cutting, but losses continued, albeit at reduced levels. At the end of the year, the UAL board approved a proposal for employees to take pay cuts and forego future pay increases in return for setting up an ESOP that would own a majority of the company's stock. On July 12, 1994, the new company began. A huge cash dividend was paid to facilitate the ESOP financing. The old management, much disliked by employees, was ousted, and new managers were hired. Today, United is the world's largest employee-controlled airline. Except for flight attendants, virtually all union and non-union employees, including those overseas, participate in the airline's ownership, though about 45 percent of the stock is still held by the general public. Since the reorganization, the price of UAL stock has nearly tripled, roughly in line with broad market averages. The company has moved solidly into the black and its business has grown substantially.

7

Conclusion

By virtually any generally accepted measure, American public schools have declined in efficiency over time, and teach students less than in many other far poorer countries. Though there are many causes, part of the problem is the perverse effect of a largely monopolistic delivery system with few incentives for excellence and efficiency. For-profit schools operating in a competitive environment that are owned in whole or part by the professionals who run them could be a promising alternative, certainly worth experimenting with.

Following the model of Employee Stock Ownership Plans (ESOPs), teachers and other employees would gain incentives to satisfy customers while containing costs. Existing school districts would become funding mechanisms providing scholarships (vouchers) to students, who would pay tuition at the school of their choice. Such schools would make profits by reducing costs through increases in efficiency and/or by expanding revenues through offering superior education products. While the transition problems are important and real, they can be overcome. At the very least, a carefully designed trial of this approach deserves strong consideration.

For-profit education already exists and is growing rapidly in the United States. It seems to work, judging from the increased demand by consumers for the services of such providers. Historically, we see that public education was adopted under pressure from special interest groups, and that its role in spreading literacy and knowledge in America has been exaggerated. Existing private schools, many of them operating for-profit, were displaced by massive government subsidies to the public school competition. It appears that the for-profit model may have been discarded too hastily.

Perhaps the time has come to revisit that earlier form of education provision that was making America into a literate nation long before the common-school movement had taken hold.

Notes

[1] See my "Small Classes Are Better For Whom?" *Wall Street Journal*, June 7, 1988, or my "The Three 'Ps' of American : Performance, Productivity, Privatization," Policy Study No. 134 (St. Louis: Center for the Study of American Business, Washington University, October 1996).

[2] Perhaps the scholar who has most extensively evaluated international differences in learning is Harold W. Stevenson. See, for example, his *The Learning Gap: Why Our Schools are Failing and What We Can Learn from Japanese and Chinese Education* (New York: Summit Books, 1992). For a recent assessment of the Third International Mathematics and Science Study, see Stevenson's *A TIMSS Primer* (Washington, D.C.: Thomas B. Fordham Foundation, July 1998).

[3] Chester E. Finn, Jr. has particularly documented the failures of U.S. schools and the poor trend in performance over time. See, for example, his *We Must Take Charge: Our Schools and Our Future* (New York: Free Press, 1991). See also his book with Diane Ravitch, *What Do Our 17-Year Olds Know?* (New York: Harper & Row, 1987).

[4] John H. Bishop, "Is the Test Score Decline Responsible for the Productivity Growth Decline?" *American Economic Review* 79 (1), March 1989, pp. 178–197.

[5] These and subsequent test statistics are all from the National Center for Education Statistics, *The Condition of Education:1998*, available on the Internet at http://nces.ed.gov/pubs98/condition98/98013.pdf.

[6] The calculations in Figure 2 involve "deflating" current expenditure per pupil data as reported in various editions of the U.S. Bureau of the Census, *Statistical Abstract of the United States* by the GDP price deflator, the broadest measure of inflation. Slightly slower growth would be reported using the Consumer Price Index; the use of a CPI modified to reflect the estimated overstatement of inflation as reported by the Boskin Commission would show a growth in spending greater than reported. On the problems with the CPI, see Michael J. Boskin, Ellen R. Dulberger, Robert J. Gordon, Zvi Griliches and Dale W. Jorgenson, "Consumer Pric-

es, the Consumer Price Index, and the Cost of Living," *Journal of Economic Perspectives* 12(1), Winter 1998, pp. 2–26.

⁷ Again, for technical reasons the numbers, if anything, are biased toward understating the U.S. spending differential with respect to major industrial countries. Specifically, exchange rates are used to convert spending in other countries into dollars. Exchange rates reflect transactions in goods traded between countries, and exclude non-traded goods. The use of the "purchasing power parity" approach would increase U.S. spending relative to most industrialized foreign countries.

⁸ Roughly 90 percent of participants in private voucher plans in Milwaukee, San Antonio and Indianapolis cited educational quality as the primary reason for selecting their private school. See Andrew Coulson, *Market Education: The Unknown History* (New Brunswick, NJ: Transactions Publishers, 1999), p. 262.

⁹ See, for example, James S. Coleman, Thomas Hoffer, and Sally Kilgore, *High School Achievement: Public and Private Schools Compared* (New York: Basic Books, 1982), and John Chubb and Terry Moe, *Politics, Markets and America's Schools* (Washington, D.C.; Brookings Institution, 1990).

¹⁰ Coulson, *op. cit.,* pp. 38-51.

¹¹See T.S. Ashton, *The Industrial Revolution, 1760–1830*, Revised Edition (New York: Oxford University Press, 1964), Phyllis Deane, *The First Industrial Revolution*, Second Edition (Cambridge, UK: Cambridge University Press, 1979), or Peter Mathias, *The First Industrial Nation: An Economic History of Britain, 1700–1914* (London: Routledge, 1983).

¹² Brian R. Mitchell, *Abstract of British Historical Statistics* (Cambridge, UK: Cambridge University Press, 1962), pp. 397 and 416.

¹³ Adam Smith, *An Inquiry into the Nature and Causes of the Wealth of Nations* (Oxford: Oxford University Press, 1976), p. 760.

¹⁴ E.G. West, *Education and the State: A Study in Political Economy* (Indianapolis, IN: Liberty Fund, 1994), p. 172.

¹⁵ Ibid., pp. 157–169. West argues that literacy was at least 80 percent. Nicholas Craft puts the figure at 76 percent. See his "Forging Ahead and Falling Behind: The Rise and Relative Decline of the First Industrial Nation," *Journal of Economic Perspectives* 12 (Spring 1998), p. 195.

¹⁶ David F. Mitch, *The Rise of Popular Literacy in Victorian England: The Influence of Private Choice and Public Policy* (Philadelphia, PA: University of Pennsylvania Press), pp. 147–149.

¹⁷ Smith, *op. cit.*, p. 764.

¹⁸ Diane Ravitch, *The Great School Wars: New York City, 1805–1973* (New York: Basic Books, 1974), p. 19.

[19] West, *op. cit.*, p. 299.

[20] Lawrence A. Cremin, *American: The National Experience, 1783–1876* (New York: Harper & Row, 1980), pp. 182–185.

[21] This discussion benefits tremendously from Joel Spring, *The American School, 1642–1985* (New York: Longman, 1986), especially chapter 4.

[22] See Ellwood Cubberley, *Public in the United States: A Study and Interpretation of American Educational History* (Boston: Houghton Mifflin, 1934) and Merle Curti, *The Social Ideas of American Educators* (Patterson, NJ: Pageant Books, 1959).

[23] Carl Kaestle, *Pillars of the Republic: Common Schools and American Society, 1780–1860* (New York: Hill and Wang, 1983).

[24] Michael B. Katz, *The Irony of Early School Reform* (Cambridge: Harvard University Press, 1968), p. 218.

[25] Herbert Spencer, *Social Statics* (New York: Robert Schalkenbach Foundation, 1970). For more on nineteenth century opponents of public, see Sheldon Richman, *Separating School & State* (Fairfax, VA: Future of Freedom Foundation, 1995), chapter four.

[26] Spring, *op. cit.*, p. 52; see also Carl Kaestle, *Evolution of an Urban School System: New York City, 1750–1850* (Cambridge, MA: Harvard University Press, 1973).

[27] Carl F. Kaestle and Maris Vinovskis, *Education and Social Change in Nineteenth-Century Massachusetts* (Cambridge, MA: Harvard University Press, 1980), esp. pp. 9–46.

[28] Cremin, *op. cit.*, pp. 182–3.

[29] Probably the most authoritative estimates on home schooling enrollments are by Patricia M. Lines. Her most recent study is "Homeschoolers: Estimating Numbers and Growth," originally published in 1998 and available on the Web at http://www.ed.gov/offices/OERI/SAI/homeschool. For a summary of research on estimated enrollments, see Karl M. Bunday, "Homeschooling Has Been Growing Rapidly in Recent Years," available on the Web at http://learninfreedom.org/homeschool_growth.html. For a chart with estimated enrollment growth in the 1980s and early to mid–1990s, see National Home Education Research Institute, "Fact Sheet IIb," at http://www.nheri.org/ under research.

[30] Patricia Lines estimated the number at 700,000 to 750,000 for 1995, while Brian Ray of the National Home Research Institute estimated the number for 1996 at 1.23 million. Using 725,000 as Lines' estimate for 1995 and assuming growth of 17–18 percent in 1996, her estimate for 1996 would probably approximate 850,000. Apparently Lines and Ray agree now that the true number lies somewhere between the Lines and

Ray estimates, hence my statement that the number approximated one million in 1996. On this point, see Bunday, *op. cit.*, p. 2.

[31] Data on aggregate private and home schooling enrollments are not completely reliable. For official government estimates, see http://nces.ed.gov/pubs99/digest98/d98t003.html.

[32] "Financial Markets Value For-Profit," *Policy Note* (Columbus, OH: Buckeye Institute, September 1999), p. 1, available on the web at http://www.buckeyeinstitute.org/policy/1999_9.htm

[33] *Ibid.*

[34] *The Tesseract Group: 1999 Annual Report* (Phoenix, AZ: September 1999), p.3

[35] Daniel Golden, "Old-Time Religion Gets a Boost at a Chain of Charter Schools," *Wall Street Journal*, September 15, 1999, p. A1.

[36] June Kronholz, "Tesseract and Others March Briskly Ahead in School Privatization," *Wall Street Journal*, August 13, 1999, pp. A1, A6.

[37] For details, go to the Web site of the Ohio Department of Education at http://www.state.oh.us/proficiency/index.htm

[38] See James Coleman and Thomas Hoffer, *Public and Private High Schools: The Impact of Communities* (New York: Basic Books, 1987), and Anthony S. Bryk, Valerie E. Lee and Peter B. Holland, *Catholic Schools and the Common Good* (Cambridge, MA: Harvard University Press, 1983).

[39] Andrew Coulson, *Market Education: The Unknown History* (New Brunswick, NJ: Transactions Publishers, 1999), p. 277.

[40] Note that by design the vouchers typically cover only part of the tuition. The average recipient must add about $1,000 to the voucher to pay for tuition. Thus poor parents are clearly willing to sacrifice a great deal to improve their children's education. On the Children's Scholarship Fund, see Terry M. Moe, "The Public Revolution Private Money Might Bring," *The Washington Post*, May 9, 1999.

[41] See Jay P. Greene, Paul E. Peterson, Jiangtao Du et al., "The Effectiveness of School Choice in Milwaukee: A Secondary Analysis of Data from the Program's Evaluation," Occasional Paper, Program of Educational Policy and Governance, Department of Government and Kennedy School of Government, Harvard University, March 1997. See also Paul E. Peterson and Bryan C. Hassel, eds., *Learning from School Choice* (Washington, D.C.: Brookings Institution Press, 1998).

[42] Cecilia Elena Rouse, "Private School Vouchers and Student Achievement: An Evaluation of the Milwaukee Parental Choice Program," *Quarterly Journal of Economics* 113(2), May 1998, pp. 553–602.

[43] See John F. Witte, "Achievement Effects of the Milwaukee Voucher Program," Robert LaFollette Institute, University of Wisconsin-Madison, February 1997.

[44] If some other educational experiences are any guide, some schools would probably raise their tuition fees well above the voucher level, giving discounts ("scholarships") to those unable to pay the incremental fee. Such price discrimination is common among profit-maximizing firms.

[45] For an excellent more detailed discussion of how the presence of market discipline will bring greater efficiency to education, see Myron Lieberman, *Privatization and Educational Choice* (New York: St. Martin's Press, 1989). For a trenchant discussion of the problems with the current system of educational delivery, see also his *Public Education: An Autopsy* (Cambridge, MA: Harvard University Press, 1993).

[46] See Eric A. Hanushek, "The Evidence on Class Size," W. Allen Wallis Institute of Political Economy Occasional Paper 98-1 (Rochester, NY: University of Rochester, 1998), Richard Vedder and Joshua Hall, "Private Schools and Public School Performance: Evidence from Ohio," (Athens, OH: Ohio University Department of Economics Working Paper, 1999), Frederick Mosteller, "The Tennessee Study of Class Size in the Early School Grades," *The Future of Children* 5, Summer/Fall 1995, Tommy M. Tomlinson, *Class Size and Public Policy: Politics and Panaceas* (Washington, D.C.; Government Printing Office, 1988), or Gene V. Glass and Mary Lee Smith, "Meta-Analysis of Research on Class Size and Achievement," *Education Evaluation and Policy Analysis* 1 (1979).

[47] This problem could be reduced in a variety of ways, including using cash bonuses tied to the specific school's financial performance.

[48] This author is generally opposed to tax abatement compared with generalized tax relief on the grounds that it violates principles of tax neutrality, leading to a misallocation of resources. In this instance, however, the previously publicly owned facility did not pay taxes, so the temporary abatement of taxes for the new schools does not cause any increased misallocation.

[49] On the general issue of resources use and student performance, see Eric A. Hanushek, "The Economics of Schooling: Production and Efficiency in Public Schools," *Journal of Economic Literature* 24 (3), September 1986, pp. 1141–57, and L.V. Hedges, R.D. Laine, and R. Greenwald, "Does Money Matter? A Meta-analysis of Studies of the Effects of Differential School Inputs on Student Outcomes," *Educational Researcher* 23 (3), 5–14. In general, Hedges, Laine and Greenwald are more optimistic about training effects on learning than Hanushek. On the specific issue of the impact of salary increases on teacher effectiveness, see Michael Podgursky and

Dale Ballou, *Teacher Pay and Teacher Quality* (Kalamazoo, MI: W.E. Up-john Institute for Employment Research, 1997).

[50] See the National Center for Education Statistics, 1998 *Digest of Education Statistics* (Washington, D.C.: Government Printing Office, 1999), especially Table 28. It is available at http://nces.ed.gov/pubs99/digest98/d98t028.html.

[51] In the short run, increased competition brought about by new private schools should increase teacher salaries. On this point, see Richard Vedder and Joshua Hall, "Private School Competition and Public School Salaries," *Journal of Labor Research* 21(1), Winter 2000, pp. 161–168

[52] William C. Symonds, "For-Profit Schools: Can Private Companies Do a Better Job of Educating America's Kids?" *Business Week*, February 7, 2000, p. 68.

[53] See Arthur B. Kennickell, Martha Starr-McCluer, and Brian J. Surette, "Recent Changes in U.S. Family Finances: Result from the 1998 Survey of Consumer Finances," *Federal Reserve Bulletin* 86 (January 2000), pp. 1–29.

[54] Ibid., p.14.

[55] James Lardner, "OK, Here Are Your Options: Employee Stock Plans Are Spreading Fast - and Not Just at High-Tech Firms," *U.S. News and World Report*, March 1, 1999.

[56] See Louis O. Kelso and Mortimer Adler, *The Capitalist Manifesto* (New York: Random House, 1958).

[57] See William Greider, *One World, Ready or Not: The Manic Logic of Global Capitalism* (New York: Simon and Schuster, 1997); Jeff Gates, *The Ownership Solution: Toward a Shared Capitalism for the 21ˢᵗ Century* (Boston: Addison-Wesley, 1998); Robert Ashford and Rodney Shakespeare, *Binary Economics: The New Paradigm* (Lanham, MD: University Press of America, 1999). For an earlier, highly influential book, see Stuart M. Speiser, *A Piece of the Action: A Plan to Provide Every Family with a $100,000 Stake in the Economy* (New York: Van Nostrand Reinhold, 1977).

[58] For a brief history of UAL and United, go to the United Web site at http://www.ual.com.

Bibliography

Ashford, Robert and Rodney Shakespeare. 1999. *Binary Economics: The New Paradigm*. Lanham, MD: University Press of America.

Ashton, Thomas S. 1964. *The Industrial Revolution, 1760-1830*. Revised Edition. New York: Oxford University Press.

Bishop, John H. 1989. "Is the Test Score Decline Responsible for the Productivity Growth Decline?" *American Economic Review* 79 (1), March, pp. 178-197.

Boskin, Michael J., Ellen R. Dulberger, Robert J. Gordon, Zvi Griliches and Dale W. Jorgensen. 1998. "Consumer Prices, the Consumer Price Index, and the Cost of Living." *Journal of Economic Perspectives* 12(1) Winter, pp. 2-26.

Buchanan, James and Gordon Tullock. 1962. *The Calculus of Consent*. Ann Arbor: University of Michigan Press.

Buckeye Institute for Public Policy Solutions. 1999. "Financial Markets Value For-Profit Education." *Policy Note*, September, available on the web at http://www.buckeyeinstitute.org/policy/1999_9.htm

Bunday Karl M. 1999. "Homeschooling Has Been Growing in Recent Years." http://learninfreedom.org/homeschool_growth.html

Bryk, Anthony S.,Valerie E. Lee and Peter B. Holland. 1983. *Catholic Schools and the Common Good*. Cambridge, MA: Harvard University Press.

Chubb, John and Terry Moe. 1990. *Politics, Markets and America's Schools*. Washington, D.C.: Brookings Institution.

Coleman, James S., Thomas Hoffer, and Sally Kilgore. 1982. *High School Achievement: Public and Private Schools Compared*. New York: Basic Books.

Coleman, James S., and Thomas Hoffer. 1987. *Public and Private High Schools: The Impact of Communities*. New York: Basic Books.

Coulson, Andrew J. 1999. *Market Education: The Unknown History.* New Brunswick, NJ: Transactions Publishers.

Crafts, Nicholas. 1998. "Forging Ahead and Falling Behind: The Rise and Relative Decline of the First Industrial Nation." *Journal of Economic Perspectives* 12 (Spring): 193–210.

Cremin, Lawrence A. 1980. *American Education: The National Experience, 1783–1876.* New York: Harper & Row.

Cubberley, Ellwood. 1934. *Public Education in the United States: A Study and Interpretation of American Educational History.* Boston: Houghton Mifflin.

Curti, Merle. 1959. *The Social Ideas of American Educators.* Patterson, N.J.: Pageant Books.

Deane, Phyllis. 1979. *The First Industrial Revolution.* Revised Edition. Cambridge, U.K. Cambridge University Press.

Finn, Chester E., Jr. and Diane Ravitch. 1987. *What Do Our 17-Year Olds Know?* New York: Harper & Row.

Finn, Chester E., Jr. 1991. *We Must Take Charge: Our Schools and Our Future.* New York: Free Press.

Gates, Jeff. 1998. *The Ownership Solution: Toward a Shared Capitalism for the 21ˢᵗ Century.* Boston: Addison-Wesley.

Glass, Gene. V. and Mary Lee Smith. 1979. "Meta-Analysis on Research on Class Size and Achievement." *Educational Evaluation and Policy Analysis*, vol. 1.

Golden, Daniel. 1999. "Old-Time Religion Gets a Boost at a Chain of Charter Schools." *Wall Street Journal*, September 15, p. A1.

Greider, William. 1997. *One World, Ready or Not: The Manic Logic of Global Capitalism.* New York: Simon and Schuster.

Greene, Jay P., Paul E. Peterson, Jiangtao Du et al. 1997. "The Effectiveness of School Choice in Milwaukee: A Secondary Analysis of Data from the Program's Evaluation." Cambridge, MA: Program of Educational Policy and Governance Occasional Paper, Department of Government and the Kennedy School of Government, Harvard University.

Hanushek, Eric A. 1986. "The Economics of Schooling: Production and Efficiency in Public Schools." *Journal of Economic Literature* 24(3), September, pp. 1141–57.

Hanushek, Eric A. 1998. "The Evidence on Class Size." W. Allen Wallis Institute of Political Economy, Occasional Paper 98–1. Rochester, NY: University of Rochester.

Hedges, L.V., R.D. Laine, and R. Greenwald. 1994. "Does Money Matter? A Meta-analysis of Studies of the Effects of Differential School Inputs on Student Outcomes." *Educational Researcher* 23 (3), pp. 5–14.

Kaestle, Carl. 1973. *Evolution of an Urban School System: New York City, 1750–1850*. Cambridge, MA: Harvard University Press.

Kaestle, Carl. 1983. *Pillars of the Republic: Common School and American Society, 1780–1860*. New York: Hill and Wang.

Kaestle, Carl and Maris Vinovskis. 1980. *Education and Social Change in Nineteenth-Century Massachusetts*. Cambridge, MA: Harvard University Press.

Katz, Michael B. 1968. *The Irony of Early School Reform*. Cambridge, MA: Harvard University Press.

Kelso, Louis O. and Mortimer Adler. 1958. *The Capitalist Manifesto*. New York: Random House.

Kennickell, Arthur B., Martha Starr-McCluer, and Brian J. Surette. 2000. "Recent Changes in U.S. Family Finances: Results from the 1998 Survey of Consumer Finances." *Federal Reserve Bulletin* 86 (January), pp. 1–29.

Kronholz, June. 1999. "Tesseract and Others March Briskly Ahead in School Privatization." *Wall Street Journal*. August 13, p. A1.

Lardner, James. 1999. "OK, Here Are Your Options: Employee Stock Plans Are Spreading Fast - and Not Just at High-Tech Firms." *U.S. News and World Report*, March 1.

Lieberman, Myron. 1989. *Privatization and Educational Choice*. New York: St. Martin's Press.

Lieberman, Myron. 1993. *Public Education: An Autopsy*. Cambridge, MA: Harvard University Press.

Lines, Patricia M. 1998. "Homeschoolers: Estimating Numbers and Growth." Washington, D.C.: Office of Educational Research and Improvement, U.S. Department of Education. Web edition: http://www.ed.gov/offices/OERI/SAI/homeschool

Mathias, Peter. 1983. *The First Industrial Nation: An Economic History of Britain, 1700–1914.* London: Routledge.

Mitch, David F. 1992. *The Rise in Popular Literacy in Victorian England: The Influence of Private Choice and Public Policy.* Philadelphia, PA: University of Pennsylvania Press.

Mitchell, Brian R. 1962. *Abstract of British Historical Statistics.* Cambridge, UK: Cambridge University Press.

Moe, Terry M. 1999. "The Public Revolution Private Money Might Bring," *The Washington Post,* May 9.

Mosteller, Frederick. "The Tennessee Study of Class Size in the Early School Grades." *The Future of Children* 5 (Summer/Fall 1995).

National Center for Education Statistics, U.S. Department of Education. 1998. *Conditions of Education.* Washington, D.C.: Government Printing Office. On Web at http://nces.ed.gov/pubs98/condition98/98013.pdf

National Center for Education Statistics, U.S. Department of Education. 1998. *Digest of Education Statistics.* Washington, D.C.: Government Printing Office. On Web at http://www.nces.ed.gov/pubs99/digest98.

National Home Education Research Institute. 1998. "Fact Sheet II b." On Web at http://www.nheri.org.

Ohio Department of Education. 2000. "Proficiency Tests." On Web at http://www.ode.state.oh.us.html.

Peterson, Paul E. and Bryan C. Hassel, eds. 1998. *Learning from School Choice.* Washington, D.C.: Brookings Institution Press.

Podgursky, Michael and Ballou, Dale. 1997. *Teacher Pay and Teacher Quality.* Kalamazoo, MI: W.E. Upjohn Institute for Employment Research.

Ravitch, Diane. 1974. *The Great School Wars: New York City, 1895–1973.* New York: Basic Books.

Richman, Sheldon. 1995. *Separating School & State.* Fairfax, VA: Future of Freedom Foundation.

Rouse, Cecilia E. 1998. "Private School Vouchers and Student Achievement: An Evaluation of The Milwaukee Parental Choice Program." *Quarterly Journal of Economics,* 113(2) May, pp. 553–602.

Smith, Adam. 1976. *An Inquiry into the Causes of the Wealth of Nations.* Oxford, England: Oxford University Press.

Speiser, Stuart M. 1977. *A Piece of the Action: A Plan to Provide Every Family with a $100,000 Stake in the Economy.* New York: Van Nostrand Reinhold.

Spencer, Herbert. 1970. *Social Statics.* New York: Robert Schalkenbach Foundation.

Spring, Joel. 1986. *The American School, 1642–1985.* New York: Longman.

Stevenson, Harold W. 1992. *The Learning Gap: Why Our Schools Are Failing and What We Can Learn from Japanese and Chinese Education* . New York: Summit Books.

Stevenson, Harold W. 1998. *A TIMSS Primer:Lessons and Implications for U.S. Education, Fordham Report* (2)7, July. Washington, D.C.: Thomas B. Fordham Foundation.

Symonds, William C. 2000. "For-Profit Schools: Can Private Companies Do a Better Job of Educating America's Kids?" *Business Week,* February 7, pp. 64–73.

Tesseract Group. 1999. *Annual Report.* Phoenix.

Tomlinson, Tommy M. 1988. *Class Size and Public Policy: Politics and Panaceas.* Washington, D.C.: Government Printing Office.

U.S. Bureau of the Census. 1998 and other years. *Statistical Abstract of the United States:1998.* Washington, D.C.: Government Printing Office.

Vedder, Richard K. 1988. "Small Classes Are Better For Whom?" *Wall Street Journal,* June 7.

Vedder, Richard K. 1996. "The Three 'Ps' of American Education: Performance, Productivity, Privatization." St. Louis: Center for the Study of American Business, Washington University, Policy Study No. 134.

Vedder, Richard K. and Joshua Hall. 1999. "Private Schools and Public School Performance: Evidence from Ohio." Athens, OH: Department of Economics Working Paper.

Vedder, Richard K. and Joshua Hall. 2000. "Private School Competition and Public School Salaries." *Journal of Labor Research,* 21(1), Winter, pp. 161–168.

West, E.G. 1994. *Education and the State: A Study in Political Economy.* Indianapolis, IN: Liberty Fund.

Witte, John F. 1997. "Achievement Effects of the Milwaukee Voucher Program." Madison: Robert LaFollette Institute, University of Wisconsin.

About the Author

Richard K. Vedder is senior fellow at The Independent Institute and distinguished professor of economics at Ohio University. An economic historian and labor economist, he has authored numerous books and monographs, as well as over 200 scholarly articles. Professor Vedder's most recent book (co-authored with Lowell Gallaway) is The Independent Institute book, *Out of Work: Unemployment and Government in Twentieth-Century America*, recipient of the Sir Antony Fisher International Memorial Award and the Mencken Award. In addition, his books include *The American Economy in Historical Perspective; Poverty, Income Distribution, the Family and Public Policy* (with Lowell Gallaway); *Essays in Nineteenth Century Economic History; Variations in Business and Economic History*, and *Essays in the Economy of the Old Northwest*.

Professor Vedder received his Ph.D. in economics from the University of Illinois. He serves as a consultant to the Joint Economic Committee of Congress, and he has been a visiting professor at numerous colleges and universities, most recently serving as the John M. Olin Visiting Professor of Labor Economics and Public Policy at the Center for the Study of American Business at Washington University in St. Louis, where he researched productivity in American public education.

Professor Vedder's professional interest in education issues expanded substantially after 1987, when he was elected to the Athens (Ohio) City School Board. For the past decade, he has extensively analyzed the results from proficiency tests administered in his state, in particular analyzing the relationship between resource use, socioeconomic factors, and student learning. He has written numerous studies relating to this research, the most recent, with Joshua Hall, entitled "Private School Competition and Public School Salaries," *Journal of Labor Research*, Winter 2000.

INDEPENDENT STUDIES IN POLITICAL ECONOMY

THE ACADEMY IN CRISIS: *The Political Economy of Higher Education.* Edited by John W. Sommer, foreword by Nathan Glazer, 348 pages, $39.95 hc, $24.95 pb.

AGRICULTURE AND THE STATE: *Market Processes and Bureaucracy.* E. C. Pasour, Jr., foreword by Bruce L. Gardner, 288 pages, $19.95 pb.

ALIENATION AND THE SOVIET ECONOMY: *The Collapse of the Socialist Era.* Paul Craig Roberts, foreword by Aaron Wildavsky, 152 pages, $29.95 hc, $16.95 pb.

AMERICAN HEALTH CARE: *Government, Market Processes, and the Public Interest.* Edited by Roger D. Feldman, forward by Mark V. Pauly, 392 pages, $39.95 hc, $24.95 pb.

ANTITRUST AND MONOPOLY: *Anatomy of A Policy Failure.* D. T. Armentano, foreword by Yale Brozen, 312 pages, $19.95 pb.

ARMS, POLITICS AND THE ECONOMY: *Historical and Contemporary Perspectives.* Edited by Robert Higgs, foreword by William A. Niskanen, 328 pages, $44.95 hc, $19.95 pb.

BEYOND POLITICS: *Markets, Welfare, and the Failure of Bureaucracy.* William C. Mitchell and Randy T. Simmons, foreword by Gordon Tullock, 256 pages, $25.00 pb.

CAPITALIST REVOLUTION IN LATIN AMERICA. Paul Craig Roberts & Karen LaFollette Araujo, foreword by Peter Bauer, 214 pages, $27.95 hc.

CUTTING GREEN TAPE: *Toxic Pollutants, Environment Regulation and the Law.* Edited by Richard L. Stroup and Roger E. Meiners, foreword by W. Kip Viscusi, 294 pages, $39.95 hc, $26.95 pb.

THE DIVERSITY MYTH: *Multiculturalism and Political Intolerance on Campus.* David O. Sacks and Peter A. Thiel, foreword by Elizabeth Fox-Genovese, 312 pages, $17.95 pb.

FREEDOM, FEMINISM, AND THE STATE. Edited by Wendy McElroy, foreword by Lewis Perry, 272 pages, $49.95 hc, $19.95 pb.

HAZARDOUS TO OUR HEALTH? *FDA Regulation of Health Care Products.* Edited by Robert Higgs, foreword by Joel J. Nobel, 128 pages, $14.95 pb, $12.95 audio.

HOT TALK, COLD SCIENCE: *Global Warming's Unfinished Debate, 2nd Edition.* S. Fred Singer, foreword by Frederick Seitz, 110 pages, $24.95 hc, $15.95 pb.

MONEY AND THE NATION STATE: *The Financial Revolution, Government and the World Monetary System.* Edited by Kevin Dowd and Richard H. Timberlake, Jr., foreword by Merton H. Miller, 453 pages, $39.95 hc, $24.95 pb.

OUT OF WORK: *Unemployment and Government in Twentieth-Century America.* Richard K. Vedder and Lowell E. Gallaway, foreword by Martin Bronfenbrenner, 352 pages, $19.50 pb, $12.95 audio.

PRIVATE RIGHTS & PUBLIC ILLUSIONS. Tibor R. Machan, foreword by Nicholas Rescher, 408 pages, $39.95 hc, $24.95 pb.

REGULATION AND THE REAGAN ERA: *Politics, Bureaucracy and the Public Interest.* Edited by Roger E. Meiners and Bruce Yandle, Jr., foreword by Robert W. Crandall, 320 pages, $49.95 hc, $19.95 pb.

TAXING CHOICE: *The Predatory Politics of Fiscal Discrimination.* Edited by William F. Shughart, II, foreword by Paul W. McCracken, 396 pages, $39.95 hc, $24.95 pb.

TAXING ENERGY: *Oil Severance Taxation and the Economy.* Robert Deacon, Stephen Decanio, H. E. Frech, III, and M. Bruce Johnson, foreword by Joseph P. Kalt, 176 pages, $39.95 hc.

THAT EVERY MAN BE ARMED: *The Evolution of a Constitutional Right.* Stephen P. Halbrook, 274 pages, $19.95 pb.

TO SERVE AND PROTECT: *Privatization and Community in Criminal Justice.* Bruce L. Benson, foreword by Marvin E. Wolfgang, 372 pages, $24.95 hc.

WINNERS, LOSERS & MICROSOFT: *Competition and Antitrust in High Technology.* Stan J. Liebowitz & Stephen E. Margolis, foreword by Jack Hirshleifer, 288 pages, $29.95 hc.

WRITING OFF IDEAS: *Taxation, Foundations, and Philanthropy in America.* Randall G. Holcombe, 277 pages, $34.95 hc, $24.95 pb.

Books in Preparation

POLITICAL ECOLOGY: *Bureaucratic, Myths and Endangered Species.* Randy T. Simmons and Charles E. Kay.

THE VOLUNTARY CITY: *New Directions for Urban America.* Edited by David T. Beito and Peter Gordon.

INDEPENDENT POLICY REPORTS

ANTIDISCRIMINATION IN HEALTH CARE: *Community Ratings and Pre-existing Conditions.* Richard A. Epstein, 36 pages, $5.95 pb.

BANK DEPOSIT GUARANTEES: *Why Not Trust the Market?* Genie D. Short and Kenneth J. Robinson, 40 pages, $5.95 pb.

CAN TEACHERS OWN THEIR OWN SCHOOLS?: *New Strategies for Educational Excellence.* Richard K. Vedder, 52 pages, $12.95, pb.

CIVIL FORFEITURE AS A "SIN" TAX. Donald J. Boudreaux and Adam C. Pritchard, 32 pages, $5.95 pb.

CULTURE AND CRIME. Allan Carlson and Christopher Check, 48 pages, $6.95 pb.

FIREARMS AND CRIME. Daniel D. Polsby, 38 pages, $5.95 pb.

FIRE & SMOKE: *Government, Lawsuits and the Rule of Law.* Michael I. Krauss, 64 pages, $12.95 pb.

ILLICIT DRUGS AND CRIME. Bruce L. Benson and David W. Rasmussen, 64 pages, $7.95 pb.

MONETARY NATIONALISM RECONSIDERED. Lawrence H. White, 36 pages, $6.95 pb.

POLICE SERVICES: *The Private Challenge.* Erwin Blackstone and Simon Hakim, 44 pages, $6.95 pb.

PRISONS AND CORRECTIONS. Samuel Jan Brakel and Bruce L. Benson, 67 pages, $7.95 pb.

PRIVATIZATION IN CRIMINAL JUSTICE. Bruce L. Benson, 68 pages, $7.95 pb.

REGULATION OF CARCINOGENS: *Are Animal Tests a Sound Foundation?* Aaron Wildavsky, 44 pages, $5.95 pb.

TOXIC TORTS BY GOVERNMENT. Bruce L. Benson, 52 pages, $6.95 pb.

VICTIMS' RIGHTS, RESTITUTION, AND RETRIBUTION. Williamson M. Evers, 52 pages, $7.95 pb.

WEALTH CREATION AS A "SIN". Jonathan R. Macey, 32 pages, $5.95 pb.

WOLF RECOVERY, POLITICAL ECOLOGY, AND ENDANGERED SPECIES. Charles Kay, 35 pages, $5.95 pb.

THE INDEPENDENT REVIEW

The INDEPENDENT REVIEW: A Journal of Political Economy, edited by Robert Higgs, is the widely acclaimed, interdisciplinary, quarterly journal that features comprehensive studies of the political economy of critical public issues. Including articles, book reviews, figures, tables, and an annual index, *The INDEPENDENT REVIEW* comprises approximately 160 pages per issue. Subscriptions are $27.95 per year for individuals and $83.95 per year for institutions. International subscribers add $28.00 for shipping and handling.

For further information and a catalog of publications, please contact:

THE INDEPENDENT INSTITUTE
100 Swan Way, Oakland, CA 94621-1428
Telephone: 510-632-1366 • Fax: 510-568-6040
E-mail: orders@independent.org
Website: http://www.independent.org